# DISTURBANCES

# DISTURBANCES
## 16 VOICES IN THE SHADOWS

 Black Moss
Press
2014

Refer to the Library and Archives Canada Cataloguing in Publication

ISBN: 978-0-88753-537-6

Cover photograph: Jason Rankin

Cover and interior design: Miriah Grondin, Nikki Turner & Jason Rankin

Editing: Samie Bauder, Miriah Grondin & Nikki Turner

**Black Moss Press**

EST. 1969

Published by Black Moss Press at 2450 Byng Road, Windsor, Ontario, N8W 3E8. Canada. Black Moss books are distributed in Canada and the U.S. by Fitzhenry & Whiteside. All orders should be directed there.

Black Moss Press would like to acknowledge the generous financial support from both the Canada Council of the Arts and the Ontario Arts Council. Also thanks to the University of Windsor English Department for its support.

*for the lovers of*
*cheese*
*kittens*
*lemons*
*& all things dark*

# CONTENTS

# FOREWORD
## MARTY GERVAIS

Sixteen voices telling stories.

That's what you will hear when you open up this little book. Theirs is a chorus that at times may be a little out of sync with one another, but oddly enough, they are bound by a common and underlying theme of darkness. That isn't to suggest something mournful or negative. In a strange kind of way, it's comfortable. It's part of life, isn't it?

The writers in this book hail from the same generation. Theirs is a vision that turns the imagination to the tangible world of everyday reality, and yanks out of that darkness something vital and authentic. The message that sometimes issues from these voices is certainly disturbing. Julianne Lacroix's poem sets the stage for this with these opening lines: *When her youngest brother is found dead/This is when the abuse makes its way to her...* Or you find Samie Bauder's highly lyrical poem drawing you into a peculiar darkness with: *roll off the bed into my dream and I'll carry you with me/drowning in lilac chains and violet crowns/the sea of flowers drifting endlessly.* Kaitlyn Gillard then reflects upon a childhood accident: *Police say that I was conscious the entire time, but I recall 'coming to' in the ambulance, asking what happened...The next thing I remember is the weight of the gauze covering half of my face. It was constantly replaced from being too heavy with blood. This is what my nightmares would later consist of. Curious, my tongue explored my mouth. The entire lower jaw had collapsed backwards so that I could not feel a row of teeth. The upper jaw remained sturdy, but my tongue mostly found holes where my teeth had been...*

Each of the writers of these stories and poems provides us with a glimpse of their worlds. Rachel Wing's portrait of Los Angeles with all the stereotypes that exist about the city of her birth differs so dramatically from Jenny Wilson's spotlight on the cultist Dutch Reform population in southwestern Ontario, or Nikki Turner's small town Ayr, Ontario. Jay Rankin's experience of crossing the border into Detroit is summed up in this: *Spotted drab-white concrete blistered with red paint shouts "liquor." A hood-hidden brute leans against the store, embers dancing in his fingertips. Rain patters against a man in a tattered coat. He shuffles to the brute, boots splashing in a puddle. He presses forward bills with shaky hands. The brute snags the cash, shoves a paper bag in the man's hands. Waves him off, mouthing "Go." I need my fix. I make my way to the store. The brute eyes me, grins, the smell of cancer wafting from his teeth...*

These are just a sampling of these 16 authors. As we turn the pages, we are invited to frolic freely in sixteen possible worlds—tough, disturbed and conflicted worlds, and more meaningfully in what Laurence Sterne described of his universe in *Tristram Shandy* as "the gutter of time." My advice, dear reader, is to take this adventure into this timeless world, and do what the photographer Ernst Haas suggests: dream with open eyes.

# EXCERPT FROM "MANEATERS"
## COLE THOMPSON

### I. STACY MALONE

*i guess i was, oh, but a dream, but a dream*

*to have thought there could ever be another james dean*

*n now i ain't nothin' but another james dream*

[...]

I've always been into older men. They've constantly proved to have more charm, more charisma. Maybe that's what drew me into my career path. I was over the boys my age— or the boys pretending to be my age with fake IDs and high school lanyards—trying to sweep me off my feet and take me home to their parents' house. I was after something bigger than that, something a little more dangerous where the only vital safety was found in their expensive apartments, their chandeliers, and their exquisite winding staircases. That was Mr. Grey for you, a man made of money and safety, and never once feared to take a treacherous walk through Hell.

I broke the number two rule when Grey rode into my life in his shiny Cadillac: never fall in love with a client. To this day I still don't know if he loved me in return, or if I had just been a player in what seemed like a twisted, surreal love story. Truth be told, I don't even want to know. I don't know if I ever did. All I know is he's dead now and it makes me happy. It also makes me cringe.

Our relationship was never simple. I had to somehow create a balance between my profession and my personal relationships—which any hooker can tell you is not easy to do. Especially when your client becomes your relationship, or whatever it was. Yet somehow I was content with our unofficial contract. I still got tied up like an object, but handled like a woman. I was still spanked like a whore, but ate dinners like a queen. And more so than anything, I was always paid for sex, but never once for kisses.

Grey was a man of mystery. He wore black suits and made eye contact that strayed like a healthy dog would into the wintertime. He was a freak. The kind of man that wore the perfect smile, the kind that pulls on the left side of your lip and releases itself back into modesty. I admired his smile and I admired the freak. He liked to put leather on and rip leather off. Never once was Grey simply casual. He didn't believe in blue jeans, only in blazers. He was, to me, the man of the century. Finger-feeding me grapes during dinnertime then pulling on my hair as he fucked me, leaving the window curtains wide open so the whole damn world could see, and just for a second, how transparent he actually was.

My life wasn't—isn't—something one would call particularly regular. It was merely a strand of one night stands and hundred dollar bills. Bills that I would spend on either Americanized Chinese food or on the latest seasonal clothing from my favourite designers. *Bills from Bill's* is what I called it. It just sounded better than "whore," but I said that too.

I was a woman, goddammit, but I was a woman of my own. I was independent and though it's cliché for a human with my parts to overspend on clothes she doesn't need, I bought them all to impress the clients I did need. From what I read about our species, about women, at least I was playing the part well; without direction, on my own fucking terms.

I did it to myself. As hard as I tried to hit the highway and run from love, I fell into its tanned, strong hands. I'd sit at dinner tables with my chin in palm and stare at him as he stared at his food; skinning lobster meat from shells and smiling at his fork. That fucking man was my James Dean, my Albert Camus. He was the man that drove too fast for the hell of it even though he had first class tickets in the pocket of his leather jacket.

So this became the life I had created. Grey paid me for business and afterwards we'd ride in his car, or on his Harley, through the city. I'd fly like a dove through the streetlights and curse at all the reds. My life was a fantasy; beautiful and intoxicating. I was the baddest bitch of the nightlife and that's a little something I don't think will ever change.

It took but six hours for my world to catch fire in the hands of Mr. Grey. After a marvelous dinner at Kuruma Zushi, it was time for business. It had started to become quite routine, actually. We'd go for dinner, depart back to our separate homes to clean up, and then I'd meet him back at his place. But things were different this time. Little had I known it was because blood didn't quite match with his beige interior needlefelt carpet.

# HERE
## JASON RANKIN

Spotted drab-white concrete blistered with red paint shouts "liquor." A hood-hidden brute leans against the store, embers dancing in his fingertips. Rain patters against a man in a tattered coat. He shuffles to the brute, boots splashing in a puddle. He presses forward bills with shaky hands. The brute snags the cash, shoves a paper bag in the man's hands. Waves him off, mouthing "Go."

I need my fix. I make my way to the store. The brute eyes me, grins, the smell of cancer wafting from his teeth.

I creak open the door. The place is dim, shadows dancing from the main source of light: the door. A fluorescent light flickers and dims, its buzz filling the room. A thin woman sits behind the cash register. Her eyes sunken, fingernails yellowed and cracked. Her veins pop out of her arms.

A ghost. I know quite a few.

I walk up the aisles. Crown Royal, Jack Daniels, Captain Morgan, Wisers, Jim Beam.... I grab a bottle of Canadian Club. The woman says nothing as I cash out—her lips trembling, eyes blank, whispering of Detroit, a sunflower sutra without Jack Kerouac.

# WELCOME TO THE AUTO SHOW
## JASON RANKIN

the media blitz has wilted and car crooks and sickle-stealing sappers take the scene

the crooks strut in their polished shoes, greasy palms flapping against their pressed pants, tightening their double-knotted ties and wiping their snot-filled noses. fingers trace up and down curves, one eye searching for the next buy to rip off a helpless family. the other eye flitting between bust and butt of the exhibition's beauties

the sappers creep around their designated targets. eyes bounce between showcase bonzos. their partners give the nod and they dive into the latest camaro, mustang, jeep, corvette. whip out measuring tapes, jotting down seat width, wheel length, the height of the pedals and even size of the lock. fingers graze against the cheap plastic doors and pleather seats, grasp a radio knob and slip it into a jacket. and they're gone and onto the next hit.

# GREEKTOWN
## JASON RANKIN

neon glow and stereo cackles whisper of athens' artisans, while the fires in the belly of pegasus remind us that gods, too, have been burned

a drunk slurs secrets, singing of streets spiralling from ashes and a sparta crushed by thebes' treachery. the city of thieves crushes the man to the curb, swimming in the spoils of its army of one-armed bandits. persia stands behind its back, watching factories crumble to dust and ignite from its five towers. macedonia buys, tries to reign financial ruin, only to shatter by winter and melt by spring

and one day greece too will be reborn in phoenix fire

# SO LONG AS IT'S BLACK
## JASON RANKIN

this. this is the place where buildings become dust. & smiles sink in the hourglass

street lit red by lights urging cars to stop. stop, here's the birthplace of the model t, the union and the $5 day. here's where a buck a beer carries men through penny pinching hours. here's where 1.8 million people flees down to 7k, leaving whispers to man a city of skeletons

this is the place. place of race riots burning dreams to ash. where business bums out as workless workers kick curb & leave town

this is the place. place of snorting 8-balls & fondling hookers. where bums take shelter in boarded buildings & fill barrels with fire

this is the place. place where dog-eyed thieves and drug-dealing hounds don't sleep. gunslingers rob shallow pockets. & shallow pockets weep for crumbs

this is the place where financial quicksand sinks a city into bankruptcy, mucks a man to the road & the product of the place rolls him down to nothing but a whisper

"this."

# HEARTLESS
## SAMIE BAUDER

Absence makes the heart grow fonder. Absence of a heart makes the fond grow richer.

Shot to the heart, but too late.

Breathing without a heart is easy. After all, the circulatory system may have a necessary coexistence with the lungs, but dependence doesn't exist either way.

Eating without a heart isn't as simple. The stomach is the key to a man's heart, they say, a kind of back door that everybody knows about but is never locked all the same. For a woman, the relationship is in no way physical and effects may vary.

A heart of gold is no better a replacement than a heart of stone, except for the level of conductivity and the malleability that may make it recyclable.

A broken heart still pumps, but squirts blood every beat, a synesthetic symphony painting a canvas of broken emotion on your sleeve.

Listen to it in your conch.

Feel it in your thumbs.

# PINK FOAM
## SAMIE BAUDER

I stared at my hands as pink murder foamed out of them, frothily ripping and broiling the skin, lesions erupting and breaking the pristine whiteness of the sink, cracking redly, sprawling fissures, burning sensory nerves through my retinas and dissolving guilt like sugar crystals in hydrochloric acid with a remainder of memories not mine.

# SIREN CALL
## SAMIE BAUDER

fall into my eyes and I'll carry you with me,
swimming in   purple wildflowers at dawn,
                a perfectionist's pixel portrait
 'til we meet again.


*we'd capture your voice in a bottle so you could whisper us to*
*sleep,*
            *silently waiving our other senses until we can*
                *taste its silky depth,*
                *feel it on our shoulders like the deep sea's pressure*
*hug,*
                *see its woven satin sine waves,*
                *smell it in the crispness of your sub-arctic air,*
*we would.*


roll off the bed into my dream and I'll carry you with me
            drowning in    lilac chains and violet crowns
                    the sea of flowers drifting endlessly,
follow me

# AURORE
## JULIANNE LACROIX

When her mother falls ill
Her stepmother steps in
When her youngest brother is found dead
This is when the abuse makes it way to her

She is beaten with an axe handle
Purple splotches pollute her skin
Broken bones cripple her
Her blood poisoned by infected wounds

Her father
Her stepmother cut off all her hair
To make the reflection of her mother disappear
They lock her up, not even the light can see her

She is burnt with an iron rod
Her siblings complain about the smell of her scorched skin
Her stepmother tells them she deserves to be punished
It is never questioned as to why

Only fed raw potatoes
She is disappearing
Her spine protrudes from her back
And her cheeks are sunken in

The doctor is suspicious
Like reading a script she lies
To prevent from getting hit again
No one does anything more to help

Eyes were as blue as the eggs of a robin
Long brown hair used to caress her face like a mothers hand
She was her mother's twin.
She is *l'enfant martyre*

# BLOODY MARY
## JULIANNE LACROIX

"I dare you"
They said
I stand in the dark,
Staring at my reflection
It's just a superstition

*Bloody Mary*

The flashlight flickers
I can feel my heart trying to escape my chest
The batteries are dying, that's all

*Bloody Mary*

I feel a cool breath linger on my neck
I turn around,
Alone
I'm imagining things

*Bloody Mary*

She stands
Nothing happens
It wasn't real
I try to leave
The door
It's locked

I turn to the mirror
Her zombielike face stares at me
Disfigured, she has come to do the same to me
I scream

*Our eyes*
*Bleed.*

# CULTURE SHOCK
## JENNY WILSON

REHOBOTH CHRISTIAN SCHOOL CLOSED DUE TO RUBELLA OUTBREAK read the headline.

Before this I had no idea what Rubella even was, but apparently it's contagious. None of the Dutch kids were coming to our school either, because they might get infected. The only reason this was happening was because they refused to vaccinate themselves or their children. It's all God's will, or something like that. Well now the whole town was getting sick, at least the Dutch Reformed and Mennonite parts of town. Which is basically the whole town.

It's like the black plague. No one has died, but still it's an epidemic. These outbreaks happen all the time in Norwich. They are all super obscure diseases that almost every baby is immunized against when they a are born. I don't know why the Dutch opt out of the immunizations, they're not herbal traditionalists or anything. I mean they drive cars and wear factory-produced clothing so they're not hippies, just part of a large religious cult. Something to do with the Bible I'm sure.

The Dutch aren't the only ones that refuse to immunize their children in our area. The Mennonites are the same. They are like the old order Amish. They live without electricity or a generator. They drive horse drawn carriages. They make their own clothing, grow and bake most of their own food. They use Clydesdales to pull the plows through their fields. They live on the back roads and only come into town when they need something from the store, which isn't very often. They wear all home made clothing The men grow long beards as a symbol of marriage. The women wear dresses that go down to their ankles and bonnets to show modesty. They're married off young and they make a living selling produce or being a carpenter. The Mennonite furniture is famous for quality and craftsmanship, and the women's cherry pies are to die for. But they're part of a cult too. A strict patriarchy under the elder's thumb.

They don't immunize their babies, and they don't go to the hospital to have them. The women sometimes die giving birth, but they refuse to ride in an ambulance or to use modern medicine. All their knowledge on childbirth is handed down from generation to generation and none of them even know how to properly sterilize all the instruments, if they even have instruments.

The girls are sometimes only thirteen or fourteen when they get married and start having children with their husbands. Of course they don't use birth control either so they pop out lots of children, who continue to grow up in the community like their parents. I have only heard of one who left.

He married his cousin when they were young. Not many Mennonites means not much wife selection. They had a baby, but because the mother had Rubella during her pregnancy the baby developed Cerebral Palsy. The Mennonites didn't know what was wrong with the girl. I heard they thought she was possessed. The Patriarch basically told the parents to let her die, but the father ended up taking the baby to a neighbour's house who drove them to the hospital. Which is blasphemous for the Mennonites. The baby girl was okay, but once the patriarch and the wife heard about what the father had done, he and the baby girl were banished from the settlement. To them it's better to be dead than to deny the old ways. He and his baby moved away after that, I think they live in Vancouver now. Talk about a cult-ure shock.

# THE CROWS EYES
## LINDSEY KISS

If we had the world
love would be no crime
We could slide up the serpent's hill
past the wandering old sky

Against night's flame
Adam would not reach us in the bush
We would gaze at the crows
a black eye for a black eye

Eve would frown on us
but our feet would be entwined
Her crawling on the ground below
would never be able to climb

Our lips stand afar from the white sanded valley
away from God's fair verse
Only will the crow hear our beats
for our drums heat the middle core

# CAMPFIRE TALES
## ELIANE DRIJBER

"Alright, while we wait for Jason to get here with the food-"

"We've already got all the stuff for smores, what more could we need?"

"S'more!"

Groans broke out at Tanya's pun. Julie waited for the clamor to die down.

"As I was saying, while we wait, how about we tell scary stories?"

"Oh, me, me! Me first! Let me!"

Tanya was practically bouncing on the wooden log which served for a bench, nearly sending Ally, who was seated on the opposite end, flying into the treetops.

"Alright, Tanya, go ahead."

Tanya abruptly stilled, leaned forward slowly, widening her eyes for effect.

"One ill-fated day...."

There was hush.

"...JULIE WAS BORN!"

Tanya rolled backwards laughing at her own joke, shouting ""Ooooooh! Buuuuurrrrrrrn!"

Julie rolled her eyes and glanced at Ally for support, "Guys, I'm serious."

"I'll tell a serious scary story."

"Oh no! Not Al-l-l-l-y! We'll just get a lecture on global

warming and starving children."

Ally glared.

"Those are serious issues, Tanya. And, quite frankly, I find them much more frightening than stupid legends about the wandering dead."

Tanya began a "blah blah blah" motion with her hand, and Julie was afraid Ally might indeed begin to give a lecture filled with dry statistics, when they were all saved by the sound of crashing bushes off to the right of the campfire.

A huge picnic basket emerged from the brush, followed by the smiling Jason.

"Hey, guys!"

The girls quickly made room on the log for Jason and his treasures.

"What did you bring?" asked Tanya.

Jason, instead of answering, bent down and opened the gargantuan wicker lid.

Gasps followed. Inside, there was a huge aluminum pot of stew, a Ziplock bag of cookies, three bags of chips, two jars of salsa, and even a twelve-pack of hotdogs hidden deep in a corner.

As the girls began to open and devour the crinkling bags of chips and cookies, Tanya stopped mid-reach into the bag of chips and asked, "Say....where's Kath-"

"SHHHH!" Julie slapped her crumb-covered hand over Tanya's open mouth. She looked over at Jason, but he was busy trying to warm up the stew over the fire.

Uncovering Tanya's mouth, Julie whispered,

"Katherine just broke up with him. Apparently he took it pretty hard."

"Holy crap...why'd they break up?"

"I don't know. She just sent me a quick text saying she wasn't coming tonight 'cause it would be too awkward, since it just happened this morning."

"This morning? Breaking up on Halloween? Isn't that unlucky or something?"

"Whatever. Just don't mention it, okay?"

"Yeah, yeah, of course."

Soon everyone was happily eating, and Julie again suggested it was time for a traditional Halloween scary story marathon.

"Oh, I've got one," said Jason.

Julie was mildly surprised, since Jason wasn't usually much of a talker, but she figured his story would be better than anything Tanya or Ally had to offer.

"Sure, go ahead, just let me grab some of this – uh... whatever kind of stew this is."

Jason smiled sheepishly, "It's beef."

"Right, cool. Ally, can you pass me a spoon? No, not the one that was on the ground!"

Once Julie was settled, Jason began.

"You've probably heard this one – I think I read it my grade nine short story textbook or something, but it's the only scary story – well, sort of scary – that I know."

He looked around; Tanya nodded encouragingly.

"Anyway. So this lady, who – I think she's pregnant – finds out her husband is leaving her or something, so she hits him over the head with a frozen leg of lamb, then she cooks the lamb leg and serves it to the police guy who's investigating her, so they never find the murder weapon."

Jason looked around again, shrugging.

"It's a lot more intense the way the book tells it."

Julie jumped in. "No, no, that was great. Pretty darn scary, when you think about it." She looked down at her bowl. "You didn't kill anybody with this beef roast, did you?"

Everyone giggled, and Jason paired a smile with another of his nervous shrugs.

"My turn!" shouted Tanya.

"Do you have a serious story this time?" asked Julie.

"Oh yeah! So, there once was this girl who got pushed off a cliff, so she haunted the seaside for centuries. She would come out at midnight and sing with the wind, and it would draw in the sailors, you know, and they would crash into the rocks and die and-"

"I think you're confused with a *siren*, from the Greek legends."

"No, Ally, this is how the story goes! Anyways, so one day this sailor is, like, sailing, and-"

Julie began to tune out Tanya's words, instead watching the effect of the flame's flickering light on the faces of her friends. Ally looked three times as grumpy as usual; Tanya looked vacant; and Jason looked like an overdone charcoal sketch.

Julie turned back to her stew, picking out the last bits of chunky, grayish meat with a broken chip. A long blonde hair clung to them, so she picked it out and threw it on the ground.

It really was too bad that Katherine couldn't come. She was such a nice girl. She and Jason had made such a great couple. It was so puzzling why they had broken up.

Julie indulged in a flashback. Katherine was leaning in to hear something Jason was telling her, her long blonde hair sliding over her ear and into Jason's face, causing him to laugh.

It was such a nice image...that long blonde hair shining in the sun....long blonde hair...

"Jason, you said this was beef, right?"

"Yep, all *cow*."

Jason smiled, and in the shadows cast by the fire, Julie saw something in his expression she had never seen in it before.

Julie looked at the last bit of sodden meat, trembling at the edge of the chip.

She suddenly retched.

# DETROIT
## HOPE GARANT

Soldier on dear Detroit
doom draws deeply near
does no one reach out to you
when you cry in the night?
its sinister sisters seeking seduction
stalking: time      money      me      you
sitting in shadows on store grounds
large bright smiling snickers
dance through bloodshot eyes
fingers grasping at bountiful breasts
give me, grab me, grope me, get me
find me, fetch me, fuck me, forget me

police sirens wail wildly
drive-bys surprise no one
and there YOU are:
alone      destitute      decayed
firefighters no longer fighting fires
poverty: the new rich
homegrown hobos hurry to hovels
discovered as dusk draws dark
hungry heaps drag themselves into survival mode
dusted doped deputies
kick in abandoned apartments
kick out hermitic homeless
to street corner cardboard cribs
"*catch me if you can*" caretakers
creep close for that extra dollar dive
renting bathrooms as bachelor bedrooms
beating big bellied beauty queens
from their tricked up teen thrones

rest worn out rambler
drifting in a hurricane of hands
in humanity's torrential storm

stop and go of shouts
wailing women, screaming babies
screeching tires and sirens squealing in the dusk
teens beating boredom by burning homes:
nightly secreted surround sound in the Dome's IMAX 3D
outside action available in every neighbourhood

# JENNIFER
## ALEX EDEN

You mumble "maybe I'll see you around"

And I say "likewise" and imagine us colliding

Into one another in a metropolis a decade from now

Where I've since gone mad from never having accomplished

Anything and you're fulfilled in every way imaginable so I plead

With you and I debase myself with welled up eyes and sacrifice all

My remaining dignity and there's an infinitesimal part of you that is

Empathetic but mostly you're ecstatic knowing you succeeded where I failed.

# GOING ON A BEAR HUNT
## KAITLYN GILLARD

Pulling my bike from the garage, I saw mom in the kitchen window. I had an urge to tell her I loved her. Of my siblings, I was the only one to miss the school bus. Mom said she'd drive me, but I would have to miss morning recess. I wanted to get to school early to tell my friend Kayla what I had alluded to on MSN the night earlier, but was unable to say. With one last look to the kitchen window, I began peddling down the street. It would have taken too long to tell my mom "I love you"

I could make up what happened as I turned onto Howard, but all I would know to be certain is that I didn't cross twice at the intersection. I stayed on the sidewalk going against traffic—probably planning to cross at the next intersection if the lights were already green. Efficiency is important when in a hurry. The construction truck blocking the sidewalk must have felt the same way with its butt to the end of 15 Cabana's driveway. I calculated how I would dodge it. *Can't go over it, can't go under it, can't go through it.* And just as I creeped to the edge of the truck, I went through it. It was an oncoming car.

I was in a hurry because I had missed the bus. My hair was oily and I couldn't pick out what to wear so I took longer than usual getting ready. I decided on a bun with fake hair extensions, sweat pants and my sister's shirt. They cut through my sister's shirt, but I still wear the sweat pants. The hair extension came undone in the accident, and as the cops approached my young body they saw the disembodied hair covered in blood and thought it was part of my scalp. A school bus drove by. When the Principal announced it later that day, classmates put two and two together. Kayla wondered what I needed to tell her, and to this day I've never known.

Police say that I was conscious the entire time, but I recall 'coming to' in the ambulance, asking what happened. To their response that I was hit by a car while bicycling, I distinctly remember telling them "No, I wasn't." Then mumbling answers of my name, where I lived, and what school I went to.

The next thing I remember is the weight of the gauze covering half of my face. It was constantly replaced from being too heavy with blood. This is what my nightmares would later consist of. Curious, my tongue explored my mouth. The entire lower jaw had collapsed backwards so that I could not feel a row of teeth. The upper jaw remained sturdy, but my tongue mostly found holes where my teeth had been and startlingly jagged teeth when there was one. My mom reassured me that they had found most of my teeth on the cement and would be able to replace them. I imagined them mistaking stones for my teeth. When they told me that I would have my jaw wired shut in surgery that night and wouldn't be able to eat solid foods for 2 months, I was glad. Maybe my face would be ruined, but at least I'd get skinnier.

When you're on hospital drugs, the wheeling into surgery is delirious. Lights go flashing by and by, and you close your eyes to stop the headache. Then you're out cold. Waking up is a different matter.

I woke up when they were pulling the blood pump out of my nose. Since they were doing surgery on my mouth, they had to pump the blood out of my stomach through my nose. Pulling a tube from your stomach to your nose hurts. In the startling pain, I realized that I could not breathe. The pump was plugging my nose. I tried to scream or tell them what was wrong, but I couldn't open my mouth. I could hear my mom's voice as I began thrashing my body around, and I thought how horrible it was that she was watching them kill me. Eventually I kicked a nurse and they gave me more drugs. When I awoke next I could explore the feeling of being unable to talk.

I stayed at the hospital for 7 days after the surgery. One of those days the nurse incorrectly placed the IV into my tissue instead of my vein. My hand filled to the size of a balloon. It now matched the other hand that was swollen purple blue from the accident.

On my last day in the hospital, I could finally walk to the bathroom with the help of my mom and the nurse. There was a mirror in the bathroom. The mirror was poor quality like the ones people hang in their lockers. It would have distorted anyone. A week of no bathing was not kind to my acne prone skin and oily hair, and it only added to my bulbous look. The stitches were a bright blue jagged line down half of my face and my teeth looked like they were covered in wiry grills. The bulky white and blue neck brace perfected my injured patient ensemble. My older brother would later ask if he could borrow the neck brace and my crutches from a previous accident for Halloween. I was my own costume.

Oral and facial surgeries persisted for years after the accident. One of these was with the plastic surgeon who denied that he had done my stitch job when he saw my face a year later. He decided he would keep me awake for his second try. I had ear phones in—now blaring extreme death metal—as I watched him take a scalpel to my face and cut it open. I was kept awake for many surgeries afterward. At least those times I could scream.

# THE SUICIDE RALLY
## KEVIN BASHAM

### I.

What drives a kid to suicide? This smoggy urban wasteland that drains the sun on gloomy days must break them like clams on an otter's gut. This city, Sarnia, so bloated with gas – it's going to pop some day. *If one of the workers fucks up, the entire city will explode.* I'm sure. How do you live with something like that hovering above you? Whether or not it's true, all of these Christmas lights will burn the holiday façade into our retinas long enough for the city to patch up any leaking smog. I'm sure.

### II.

A native girl killed herself. Eight others did the same in two years. People wondered about family issues, drunkenness, everything under the smog. I wonder about a lack of future; if you can't see five years down the road, I doubt you can see a reason to keep traveling. Might as well stop the car and let it run.

### III.

Paint this town grey, because it certainly doesn't like rainbows. Suicide is more common amongst gay teens. I never thought about how many times *gay* and *faggot* were shot around wantonly until revisiting this cesspit. Put a bullet in the same wound a thousand times and tell me if it's still bleeding. And if it's gangrenous, kids say just cut it off at the head; let all the blood sink to those swinging toes. Sorry, I gave the city a bad palette. It likes red too.

## IV.

I've lived in this city for most of my life; nothing's changed. Elders take those last minute leisure walks before night falls. They tell their kids to defend themselves if they get punched at school, and tell them to accept Jesus in the same breath. Black and white don't exist here: the air is grey.

## V.

And God damn it if I don't think it's my fault somehow. You'd think they'd call their friends, but they don't. Maybe they're too scared to call—afraid of being treated like cattle, shipped off to the psych ward. I want to uproot your tombstone, drag you out of the grave, and ask why. I know there isn't a why.

## VI.

The suicide rally is what got me. I advocated against it. It was created by my high school, and held in the gymnasium. A pack of kids hollering for change at each other – the people who were stable to begin with. Many were the bullies who ruined high school for other kids: now they care? I saw a lack of empathy, and a bandwagon of life supporters, and ego boosting. They created a petition to prevent suicide, and it was signed by the attendees. Sign your name, save a life. I'm sure.

Just think how shallow that ink sunk into the page – if you want to save a drowning person's life, you need to get your arms wet at least.

## VII.

I know a guy whose friend killed himself. He was hurt by it, badly. I haven't spoken to him since. I know a woman whose mother tried to commit suicide. She attacked me for disagreeing with the rally. I'm just an outsider to them—the eternal opposition of good, I'm sure. The kind of egotistical scumbag that thinks his opinion is worth something. The kind of person that the world would be better without.

Throw me in the fire, watch me burn, make me a scapegoat. Embers die in time.

# SIREN SONG
## RACHEL WING

Every night in my city I heard sirens.
I say 'my city' but I mean
my town.
2 and a half blocks off the main road
and I could hear the cars
racing.
Could count them
one
two
three
Fire truck.
I learned the sounds.
They were always heading west.
East is where LA ends
and LAPD ends with it.

On the phone with someone
I paused mid-
sentence
as the sirens blared
and faded
west.
"What?"
Nothing. Just sirens
"Sirens aren't
nothing"
I hear them every night
"That's impossible."
He wasn't from around
here.

I moved. New city.
New sirens.
Now I fall asleep to the sounds of a bridge.
Horns honking,
trucks downshifting
and it's too cold for crickets.
But
every now and then a siren
blares
and fades west
and it sounds like home.

# ALMOST HOME
## RACHEL WING

Do you remember how we fought
over where we would live
when *then* was *now?*
We grumbled and muttered
we stuck out our tongues,
tossed insults at cities,
both of us too young to compromise.

LA was the city you fought for
and I'd roll my eyes and wonder how
you could want a city like this one
when the world was so full
of so many others.
You were never interested in
others.

I am certain I had reasons back then
for wanting to leave the city that raised me.
Fifteen year old girl reasons,
logical, sound
right.
But they seemed to disappear
when you were already long gone.
I can't even remember them anymore.

I don't know if you saw the beauty of the city
or if you just saw a home.
I didn't see it
or maybe I just needed to be shown.

But when I see it now I think of you and wonder
what reasons you had and how you're enjoying those
other cities.
When I see it now and can't imagine leaving
I think of you and wonder if you remember
the home we almost had.

# SCHOOL NIGHTS*
## MARK ORIET

With a bowl of Lays chips
I could watch *Animal Planet* for hours.
I'd lay flat on your couch
Getting up only to make sure
The cats had water in their bowl,
And I would lie
Late in the night
To the Gulf of Kenya
With my head on your lap
And the Tigers beating up the Zebra
The entire time.

---

\* An inhabitation of *Twilight Cincinnati* by Robert Earl Stewart

# TAKING UNDER
## KATERINA STAVRIDIS

dusty skylines
and signs: *Enter at Your Own Risk*
abandoned

stained with blood, dried tears, and ash
the streets whisper with flames and smoke,
secrets locked away with rubble and lost children
as winter takes more time and life,
heat defeated and exiled, again
damaged bodies will have to wait

a room where
an elegant piano lies on its side in the dust
smiling with broken teeth, and
the sun struggles through tense air
and peppers the obscure wood

desolation
it sleeks between the decaying trees,
it slithers through the chimneys
to wipe-out persistent light, and
enters through the nose and mouths and souls
of stubborn beasts
turning dreams into nightmares

buildings melt into sharp edges,
the glass re-forming to sand,
crab grass between the cracks,
the suit and tie walks by *bro-ken,*

a dog rolled onto her back giving us a gravity smile

**OTOR CITY** crumbles onto cinders
as walls stand alone and listen
to inevitable sirens and sighs,
as snow floats to the pavement
red wearing streets shiver
bearing the white flag

# THE LOYALISTS
## KATERINA STAVRIDIS

standing at attention
skinny, white, naked in snow
all imperfect scars
visible
vulnerable
diseased
the limbs shiver in brisk winds.
deep gashes and knots -
evidence of old age, yet
they hold their ground,
in salute,
but only one with memories
      secrets
      sex
      love
a loyal, strong patriot,
no struggle when a switchblade
carves names and a heart,
winter-blows and bomb-chills
do not discover surrender


smoke dancing around the
flashing lights on peeling bark
illuminate the shell shocked birches

# AND SHE SMILES
## KATERINA STAVRIDIS

you wait until the light is dim
her curves and corners gleam better that way,
sitting patiently in the middle of the room
she silently beckons,
*come closer*

stroking her smoothness you
remember how sweetly she sings,
lifting up her cover, she smiles
a set of gleaming pearls
in shadow

the moment before contact is peaceful,
she is patient

the first touch sends
a low hum into the air,

trembling now
you press down 6 of 88

faster and out of time
she keeps up

silent when you finish, you push away
from her dampness,
she waits until you return to her feet
and she smiles
pianissimo

# AVENUE
## MIRIAH GRONDIN

"Yuh fu'ing pig-assed bitch who the fuhhh're you."

"Who pays, Buck? Huh? Who? Sit on your fucking ass all day drinking beer. Have another one. Help your fucking self. Why don't you get a fucking job? Huh? You fucking..."

"Shuttafuhhh up. Fu'ing stupid whore. Your ma don't even love ya, look how much she comes around ya fat cu..."

I slam the window. Pupils adjust to the night as a soft green glow bathes the room. 3:27. Rolling on my stomach, I fold the curtains over one another and set them so only my eyes are uncovered. Squinting through cotton binoculars, I can make out the slivered moon's light on the pool water next door. The darkness tints the water, as if the pool swallowed the moon. A faint light gleaming through the surface like a flashlight pressed to palms, illuminating skin-trapped blood. The moon trapped in blueberry gelatin.

There's a pause and the wooden gate crashes. She slams it again. Again. Her arm swinging like a batter taking practice hits. I catch her shape around the corner of the pool. I wait for the ignition. Wait. No, it's his shape. Big black floating blob. Gravel crunch. Meep. Fvrrroom.

"Who fucking paid for it? Huh? My fucking money. My car."

"Shut't fuhhh up fat ass."

"Get the fuck out. Get out. Out. Fucking asshole."

I don't see her move but I hear her yank the door handle like rapid-fire. He gets out. Door slams. Gate slams. Shapes dart around the pool. I can only see the moon now, trapped in its water cage, jittering rapidly. The water must be chilly.

"You think I'm gonna let you fucking have these beers? Fuck you. They're mine just like that damn car. Just like this damn house."

"Fu'ing rental fat ass."

"You get fired cause you fucking can't shut your mouth."

"Uhn. Shut the fuhhh up."

A noise comes from the deck, something like sandpaper rubbing together. I shift, trying to connect eyes with image with sound. The curtains fall, my drapery binoculars busted. Splash. Holy crap he's thrown her in the pool. Pssshhhh. Slap cotton to my face and stare. It wasn't her she's on the deck. Where's he? A box in her hands she chucks it overboard like excess cargo from a sinking ship. Twenty-four bottles rattle before they're swallowed and I can't see the moon.

"Fuh... fu'ing kiddin' me."

A bigger splash. Someone's in the water, their feet trampling the moon, the water billowing in ringlets, radiating. He's lifting the soggy box. It splits as he reaches the wooden sides and the bottles clutter the deck. He shoves them and lifts himself, sloshes onto land. The bottles shatter on concrete, our fence. Please not my car. I let the curtains droop unfolding my binoculars.

I curl, knees pressed against my shirt, hands gripping my shins. My shirt sticks to my chest from the rising heat of the closed window. The sound of more slurs seep through the double hung glass, bottles shattering like shrapnel on concrete. I sync my eyes on the clock. Is Sage inside? She's too young to have left. Des took off a year ago. Outside their voices pick up. 2 a.m. three nights a week. It's a school night. Like the nights I used to fall asleep and wake at 8 a.m.

for school. We'd walk home with five-cent candies from the corner store. If you bought enough they couldn't make you count, they had to take your word for it, so we always got more than we paid for. We'd race home and on every lawn were parents and kids – Renée playing with Tips while Ms. Janie tended her shrubs, the six Samson siblings down the block waving from their bikes. Des, Renée, and Sophie, the middle Samson kid, running over to my lawn.

"What're we gunna play today, Vics?"

"I dunno, Sophs! How 'bout Polly's? I'll trade you."

"We're playing hunters."

"Ren, you picked last time. Not fair. How 'bout we have a BB Club meeting?"

"You're not in the club, Des. You gotta have twenty Beanie Babies. I told you and you only have nineteen."

"Mom said. I'm in the club she said so. I'm telling."

"Des, you can have my Puddles then you can come. How 'bout we play house?"

"Thanks, Vics. See, Ren."

"Whatever, we're playing hunters. I'm the Wolf Queen. Then I'm teaching you guys to skateboard."

We never did learn to skateboard. Me and Des found it more fun to ride the boards down the sidewalk on our stomachs. We were belly surfers not skaters. But Ren didn't like that and fought with Des. Des tripped over our bike pile and cut her leg. We all cried except Ren. She laughed. Ms. Janie grounded her for a week. The grounding lasted a day which felt like a week, to us. We vandalized the sidewalk and tried to make a world record for the longest hopscotch. We got down to the end of the block before it rained and washed that day's dreams away. We set up the sprinkler in the summer and Ren peed in the centre. Ms. Janie grounded her. Again. Soph's mom decided Ren was a bad influence and banned her from playing with us. We'd see each other on opposite sides of the road and wave. We'd sneak letters into Soph's window with secret instructions on where to meet and she'd tell Mrs. Tina she was going to Des's. We'd spend the afternoon in the pool Ms. Janie bought Ren. Waves and whirls. Our feet slapping the concrete as we ran to the house to pee. We didn't think much of the slippery slabs that—

"I fucking want a divorce. Yeah, I said it. I WANT A DIVORCE."

"Yuh fuhhhing thin' I care?"

I blink and there's the clock. 4:56. My shirt is drenched. In the morning, their pool will be iced with shredded cardboard and deck chairs, my driveway decorated with shattered brown and empty aluminum. Their gate will hang crooked on the hinges and the car will be gone.

White blotches float across my room. I blink. Light distortion of sleep-sober eyes. I peel my shirt off. Aim the fan at my face. Fall on my pillow. Can't blink away blobs. They dance. To my blink rhythm. Blink desk. blink dresser. blink mirror. Voices break outside. Little voices muddle in my head. I lay. Blobs bob. Just me and the blobs. Roll over. Pull curtain. I see the moon. Shut my eyes and all I can see is the sidewalk.

# THE SWAN
## NIKKI TURNER

I didn't grow up in Detroit. I could count the number of times I'd heard sirens on one hand. I was not afraid to walk the streets, to talk to strangers. There was no arson, homelessness, not even poverty. I didn't grow up scared, or unhappy. I didn't have a curfew, or rules. I just lived and did whatever I wanted to. I was never boxed in, not in Ayr.

Nothing was scary in Ayr. Even the cemetery filled with graves and wilted, dead flowers possessed some serene beauty. It could be a bit boring when no matter which way I turned, I was taking the scenic route. There wasn't much of an escape from the picturesque.

There was the pond, in the middle of Centennial Park, with the beautiful wooden bridge and the golden gazebo at its end seen through the blowing willow trees. Walking through the park, feeding the pure white swans bits of my ice cream waffle cone was one of the few reoccurring pastimes I can remember. Beautiful, but unsatisfying.

I grew a penchant for adventure, for horror. Most of my obsession started at the local video store. The owner knew my mom so as long as I brought a note of permission, I was allowed to rent any R Rated movie. I tried so hard to be scared, but movies were just movies and I couldn't believe the outcomes to be true. They just didn't affect me in the way they were supposed to.

My parents thought I was a little bit weird and had a few concerned phone calls from the school when I started reading every book I could about the Blair Witch and studying Wicca instead of Math. To my mom and dad, I was just going through a phase.

Some friends and I grabbed my parent's video camera, walked the two minutes from my house to the cemetery, and created a horror movie behind all the grave stones. But alas, the graves in Ayr had such a calming effect. It wasn't the right scene for any Horror film. My neighbours, however, did provide the perfect scene.

All year round, their house was dubbed "The Haunted House," even though the decorations were only set up for about two weeks. I tried to get involved with the decorations as much as possible, but I was young and couldn't do much. When I got a bit older, my neighbours stopped decorating for Halloween. Julie, my neighbour, was diagnosed with a brain tumor, which meant that she and her husband had to focus on her health and I knew it was time to get my kicks elsewhere.

I didn't grow up in Detroit, but neither did my other next-door neighbours. They were curious. They were the kind of Catholics that saw Halloween as a night of devil worship and in protest to its celebration, turned off their lights and shuttered themselves from the wee monsters, super heroes and princesses. My parents never liked them very much, and if ever they were concerned about my safety, it was because of them.

Their son was about ten years older than me and he had always been a rebellious teen. From a young age, I remember hearing heavy metal coming from the quaint cookie cutter house next door, followed by yelling and door slamming. I don't know what happened beyond what I could hear from my backyard, but I do know that things changed. He changed.

His parents were so proud of him. It was the day he found God. The day God found him. They talked and talked and God asked so much of him, to prove his faith. I didn't know why at the time, but he was sent away. My parents told me he was sick when I asked why he wasn't at home anymore.

"Like a cold?"

"Yes, exactly."

He came home every weekend, escorted by two men dressed all in white. Just for twenty-four hours. He would stay all of Saturday and would be picked up after dinner on Sunday night. On these days home, I would watch him from the front window. I would time it from the moment I saw him leave the house to the moment I saw him re-enter. It became a sick and mysterious game for me. I wanted to know what he was doing on those two hour walks. Even taking the most scenic of the scenic routes in Ayr still didn't take two hours.

I watched him leave one Sunday, drawing with chalk on my driveway, and waited for his return. He took longer than usual and when he finally walked into my field of vision, he wasn't alone. He was waving a white flag above his head as if he was surrendering. But as he got closer, I noticed the white was stained with red. I went inside and told my parents.

When I looked outside to my neighbour's later that night, the white clothed men were there alongside the police. I never saw any of them again.

But there was the image of surrender that felt engraved in my eyes. The pure white swan, stabbed through with a sharpened stick above my neighbour's head as if he was the leader of God's parade. I didn't sleep for a week.

I didn't grow up in Detroit, but I did end up on its South Shore. Filled with all the thrills and realistic horrors I'd always dreamt of. Once, I witnessed this beautiful orange glow out past Ambassador Bridge. I watched for twenty minutes before I realized it was a fire. I immediately wished I hadn't.

The first time I entered Detroit was just in passing. I was headed to the airport to fly out to Washington. My friend was driving and we got lost. We were on the highway, and then we were on side streets, a rusted metal fence, a charred house, the biggest pothole I had ever seen. Having heard horror stories of car jackings, men opening driver's side doors with guns in hand, car still running, my friend only just slowed when approaching the red octagons.

We admitted after a while just how lost we were and stopped at a convenience store to ask for directions. For a first experience with the apparently scary Detroit, this was uneventful. A small convenience store, just like the ones in Windsor, just like the one in Ayr. It was boring. Disappointing.

Inside was this kid, in a plastic box. Or, I guess a bullet-proof box. The only employee of the store was separated from everything. Safe, in his little box.

The prepubescent teen looked as bored as any young convenience store worker. His white uniform with the red stripes hung off him loosely, as if he had worn it in for a long while. I was probably only two or three years older than this kid, who was working a job so unsafe he was hidden in a box. We asked him for directions and went on our merry, safe way. But he wasn't safe. Not once he left that box.

I didn't grow up in Detroit. But this kid did.

**VOICES IN THE SHADOWS** BY JASON RANKIN

From the left: Marty Gervais, Katerina Stavridis, Julianne Lacroix, Eliane Drijber (back), Lindsey Kiss (front), Samie Bauder (back), Nikki Turner (front), Rachel Wing (back), Cole Thompson (front), Kevin Basham (back) Miriah Grondin (front), Mark Oriet, Alex Eden, Jenny Wilson (back), Jason Rankin (front) Kaitlyn Gillard and John B. Lee.

# AUTHOR BIOS (IN ORDER OF APPEARANCE)

**COLE THOMPSON** enjoys writing about NYC and hookers, even though he's never been to New York and has never paid for sex. Besides that one time.

**JASON RANKIN** would have told you about himself, but his cat ate the script.

**SAMIE BAUDER** cements abstraction and twists her words into bow-tied butterfly knots.

**JULIANNE LACROIX** is from a small town in Middle of No Where Northern Ontario. She has never been good at filling out the "about me" sections of websites. She is no better at writing this author bio.

**JENNY WILSON** takes inspiration from the true abnormal situations around her that might be stranger than fiction

**LINDSEY KISS** may float away on topics and discourse, but beyond all, her poems take readers to a new isle.

**ELIANE DRIJBER** has red hair and is human, supposedly. She writes stuff sometimes.

**HOPE GARANT** writes about life, because she's too busy to have one.

**ALEX EDEN** composes stories often influenced by television and film, and characterized by their nihilism, hopelessness and ambiguity.

**KAITLYN GILLARD** — when asked by the paramedics who she was, where she lived, her name... She mumbled "no, i wasnt." Kaitlyn can be found cycling around Michigan and Ontario.

**KEVIN BASHAM** writes about the mythical, the disgusting, and anything that shouldn't be said in public.

**RACHEL WING** writes because it's much less expensive than a therapist.

**MARK ORIET** very much likes herbal teas, and can be found frequently scouring the shelves of his home town's Shoppers Drug Mart for sales on his favourite brands.

**KATERINA STAVRIDIS** writes because no one knows what she's talking about otherwise.

**MIRIAH GRONDIN'S** author bio is lost under a slush pile of her own descriptive prose. She hopes to find it once the snow melts.

**NIKKI TURNER** writes for the sole purpose of embarrassing her family. Is it working?